The Queen's Rules

Rules,
Decrees,
Directives &
Proclamations
For Every Woman
Who Is or Will Be
Queen

Marva Dew

PUBLISHED BY FIDELI PUBLISHING, INC.

ISBN: 978-1-948638-80-7

PUBLISHED BY

Fideli Publishing, Inc.
119 W. Morgan St.
Martinsville, IN 46151

www.FideliPublishing.com

Dedication

This book is dedicated to Sister Queens everywhere — every woman & every young girl who desires to be Queen and use the Word of God and godly wisdom to enhance, empower, and enrich her life. Queen, I encourage you to live a life that will bring glory & honor to God. May you reign with Him in this life and in the life to come is my humble prayer.

Crown On Queen!
~ Marva Dunn

Table of Contents

Acknowledgements

P raise be to God — King of Kings and Lord of Lords! It is God alone who rightfully deserves all praise, glory, and honor. I am thankful every day for His saving grace and redemptive power. It is because of His grace and mercy that I am able to walk this walk and claim the title and authority of Queen. What A Mighty God We Serve!

I thank God for the Queens in my life. First and foremost, Mrs. Margaret Louise Ceaser (deceased), my beloved mother and my Original Queen who raised me to be a true Queen. She modeled Queenship before me and for that I am eternally grateful. My Sister-Queens: Rose, Sharon, Sandra, Rene´ (deceased), and Alicia; and my Sister-Sisters, Joyce, Tiona, and Janice who have walked this journey called life with me along with my loving sisters-in-love: Dara, Charissee, Tara (deceased), and Joyce; my daughter, Eboni; my daughter-in-love, Omega; and my beautiful granddaughter, princess Lavender Grace. I am grateful to each of you for being my family and an intricate member of my "tribe". To my nieces, cousins, and every female member of my family—I see you Queens and I love and appreciate you.

To my Antioch Missionary Baptist Church family of sisters—you have allowed me to learn, teach, train, and develop sisterhood on a level I never thought possible. Thank you for embracing not only me, but the very idea of united Christian sisterhood. May we forever be Sisters For Sisters working to ensure that "Every sister will be a sister and every sister will have a sister; so that no sister will stand alone!" Much love to my young "Queenettes" who are working and developing into Queens before my very eyes. Thank you for allowing me to personally pour into you. Whenever I call for you, it still amazes me that you continue to show up—focused and ready to listen and apply God's wisdom. Follow the rules Queenettes! I am with you and as always—I am watching you.

To the Ministers' Wives and Widows from near and far who share with me both the blessings and burdens of standing beside the men who stand at the helms of God's great churches, thank you for being the rocks upon which I sharpen myself. May we take hold of our Queenship and then enlarge the borders of the minds of those within our sphere of influence. Thank you to my personal mentors: Criss Lott, Alma Brasfield, and Regina West. I tip my crown to my Sister-Queens: Molifenge Walker, Rebecca Robinsson, and Janeen James. To Queen Doniella Ligon—you are a true purpose-pusher and one of the most loving and giving WINers I know. To my Sister-Queen-Friends from childhood: Countess Price, Dawne Biggs, and Donna

Estevez—thank you for loving me and standing with me down through the years—you are my sisters. I respectfully acknowledge one of the strongest Queen Tribes I know: Arlene Jones, Tracy Jackson, Sheila Thompson, and Bridgette Moran. You Queens take sisterhood to another level. Yvette Faye Black, you were born to be Queen and I thank you for being my VBFITWWW (Queen Code).

To the men in my life: my father: Nelson Paul Ceaser (deceased); my brothers: Joseph, Nelson (deceased), and Michael; my son, Samuel; and my brothers-in-law John and Albert—thank you for standing the watch in my life—ensuring that I grew and developed into the Queen I am today. To my strong and courageous nephews, cousins, and every male member of my family—God has blessed me mightily with and through each of you. Maxentius John, you are my forever friend and I thank God for you. Men of Antioch, thank you for being the men of substance and valor necessary for Queens to look upon with respect and honor.

I am most grateful to the one true love of my life, my beloved husband, friend, and partner—Reverend Dr. Gerald M. Dew—my chosen earthly King. Thank you for your unending, uncompromising, unconditional love. It is my forever joy to share this life with you. You tell me every day how much you love me; and then you go about proving it. My love for you will never end and I shall forever reign as your Queen!

Finally, to every Sister-Queen, may the teachings in this book serve as a source of enrichment, empowerment, and encouragement as you move forward in faith with the absolute assurance that though we are Queens in this lifetime, one day God Himself will crown us for all eternity. When we all get to heaven, what a day of rejoicing that will be.

Blessings,
Marva Dew

Introduction

As a child I hated my name, "Marva", who names a child that? I never saw it on the fancy bracelets hung in the stores; never printed on mugs; and never heard it repeated by Miss Sally Claster as she peered through her looking glass and called out the names of smart obedient preschoolers on the 1964 children's television show Romper Room. No matter how closely I sat to our floor model television and frantically waved my arms, she never saw me—never called my name. Therefore, I believed my name had no meaning, no purpose, and no beauty. I was invisible.

But my mother saw my invisible self. She somehow knew what I needed most. I needed something to believe in—something to strive for. My mother soon called for something that would change my life, she insisted her daughters be ladies. Charm school was my saving grace and my secret passion. I loved everything there was to love about being a young lady—etiquette classes were my favorite times of learning. I loved learning how to talk, walk, serve, and navigate life as a lady. I would practice setting the table for 8, the proper handshake for a lady, how to sit, and when to stand. These lessons brought me great joy. I became a master of proper etiquette. Emily Post's etiquette books were my bedtime stories and my daytime orders. Being a lady was non-negotiable. I was determined to be a refined, graceful woman of class.

As I matured into a young woman, a strange phenomenon began to take effect. I found myself shying away from my true calling. I would purposefully water myself down so that others would feel better about themselves. Beautiful, smart, creative, graceful, lovely—those words were like nails on a chalkboard to me. They caused me to shy away from life because others used those attributes as weapons against me. I found myself misunderstood by family, friends, associates, and even strangers. I would hear their remarks, "Who does she think she is? Marva thinks she's so much? Who cares Marva if we sit with our elbows on the table or eat spaghetti with our fingers? Marva how silly can you be to want lace handkerchiefs for Christmas." And so I learned to smile. I learned to cover up my true feelings. I learned to silence my true voice. At times I even practiced the disgusting habits of spitting on the ground or slurping my soup when eating just to fit in. I became what others expected me to be—just plain old invisible Marva. I became everyone's favorite friend. And that was my life, my norm—and I was fine with that.

Many years later out of shear boredom I began to read my grandmother's old ragged Bible. I read about this magnificent God. I was amazed by Him. Although Catholic, I began to attend a Baptist Church where this young, exciting preacher (Reverend Gerald M. Dew) talked about this same God in a way that made my soul yearn for Him. Could it be, was it somehow possible, that God Himself would accept me? Could this mighty God somehow see even little old invisible me? The more I heard of and read about Him, the more I wanted to know. I came to believe God and His Word. I accepted Him as my Lord and Savior and came to know Him in new and exciting ways. He became more than the God of my Catholic School catechism teachings. It was hard to believe that His Word was talking to and about me, but I kept reading, hoping, and trusting. And over time and through faith I came to know that He really does love and accept me just as I am. I came to know that I really am fearfully and wonderfully made. I came to know and believe that God is with me. I came to know that God has a plan and a purpose for MY life. God's Word transformed me and changed my way of thinking. I came to depend on Him and trust what His Word says about me. It was a gradual progression, but I slowly and meticulously began my journey in life as His child. I was determined to reflect His image. I wanted God to be proud of me. I wanted Him to see me and say my name with pride.

And then it happened, like a butterfly shedding its cocoon, I began to emerge from the safe, private cave I had built around myself for protection. I took a chance on God and decided to walk in the light of His love. I was no longer afraid of what others thought of me. As I embraced my true self I found others did too. They actually began to gravitate towards, not me, but the light of God that was within me.

As the years progressed I came to know how blessed I was to be God's child named Marva. I soon found out that my name actually means lady, mistress of the house; sage (wise); renowned friend. Over the years I have tried to purposefully live out my name for the good of others, the growth of the church and the glory of God. These things I now know... I am a woman of God. I have come into the kingdom for such a time as this. My soul makes her boast in the Lord when I say I am all-together lovely. I no longer apologize for walking in the light of God's Word. I fiercely defend the Word of God through my walk and not my talk. And so I introduce myself to you today, my name is Marva. I am no longer invisible. I am she who was destined to be Queen.

This book is a compilation of biblical principles, wisdom from my life experiences, and encouraging truths from others. They have served me well and I am convinced they will add value to your life. All scripture is from the New International Version or the King James Version of the Bible. The known author of every quote is acknowledged. I welcome you Queen to learn and apply the knowledge and wisdom found within this book. I support you as you continue your journey in life. And I celebrate you as you walk in your calling according to God's plan.

But you are a chosen people, a royal priesthood, a holy nation, God's special possession, that you may declare the praises of Him who called you out of darkness into His wonderful light."

—1st Peter 2: 9

WELCOME TO THE Queendom

...The domain over which the Queen rules

Build It • Fortify It • Protect It

Queen

/kwen/ noun
Me. You. Her. Us.

Synonyms:
Woman of God
Woman of Faith
Spirit-led Woman
Daughter of the Most High
Ambassador for Christ
God's Sanctified Representative

Queen

Know Your Position & Stand In It

Damsel:

A young woman or girl; a maiden, originally one of gentle or noble birth.

Princess:

A woman having sovereign power; a female member of a royal family; especially a daughter or granddaughter of a sovereign; one likened to a princess; especially a woman of high rank or of high standing in her class or profession.

Queen:

A female monarch; a female chieftain; a woman eminent in rank or power; a female having supremacy in a specified realm.

—Merriam-Webster Dictionary

The Queen

I have named you Queen,
There are taller ones than you, taller,
There are purer ones than you, purer.
There are lovelier ones than you, lovelier.

But You Are The Queen.

When you go through the streets
No one recognizes you.
No one sees your crystal crown.
No one looks at the carpet of red gold that
You tread upon as you pass,
The nonexistent carpet.

But You Are The Queen.

— Author Unknown

The Queen's Top 3 Rules

RULE #1

Never Be Number 2

The Queen Stands Alone

She does not battle for a position she already holds. There is only ONE Queen per Queendom. And there is no such position as Vice-Queen.

Admit It... You Were Born to Be Queen

"...And who knoweth whether thou art come to the kingdom for such a time as this?"

—Esther 4:14

The Queen's Rules & Royal Decrees

RULE #4

The Queen is a Woman—Fearfully & Wonderfully Made

"I praise You because I am fearfully and wonderfully made; Your works are wonderful, I know that full well."

—Psalm 139:14

"She is a woman. She is a mother, daughter, wife, sister. She is a person. She is strong, smart, and crafty. She is passionate, courageous, and generous. Cooking barefoot is only one of several superpowers. She is action, emotion, and devotion. She has hope, beauty, and power. She has a brain and she knows how to use it. She gives life. She gives you respect, love and gratitude. She believes in you. She will nurture you, fight for you. And she deserves nothing less from you."

—Author Unknown

"Pretty women wonder where my secret lies. I'm not cute or built to suit a fashion model's size. But when I start to tell them, they think I'm telling lies. I say it's in the reach of my arms, the span of my hips; the stride of my step; the curl of my lips. I'm a woman Phenomenally. Phenomenal Woman That's Me."

—Maya Angelou

"I am woman, hear me roar in numbers too big to ignore and I know too much to go back an' pretend… I am strong. I am invincible. I am woman…"

—*"I Am Woman" song by Helen Reddy*

RULE #5

QUEEN
It's Not Just A Word or Title.
It's A Calling! It's A State of Mind!
It's An Attitude! It's A Lifestyle!

RULE #6

The Queen is a Praying Woman
Through Prayer She Stays Connected To God—
Her Power Source

"Seek the Lord and His strength, seek His face continually."

—*1st Chronicles 16:11*

"Do not be anxious about anything, but in every situation, by prayer and petition, with thanksgiving, present your requests to God."

—Philippians 4:6

"Our most important relationship in life is our relationship with God. That relationship is strengthened through the miracle of prayer—and prayer is just that, a miracle in and of itself. Through prayer, we draw nearer to God. Our prayer life must be consistent and persistent. God desires that we talk to Him on a daily, hourly, minute-by-minute basis. He wants to hear from us personally. Our prayer life, our connection with God, will sustain us when nothing else will. Prayer is simply talking to God; believing that He hears us; and knowing that He will move on our behalf. Just a little talk with God really does make things right."

—Marva Dew

"When God's warriors go down on their knees, the battle is not over, it has just begun."

—Author Unknown

"Nothing in my nature is a Godly woman. So every morning I have a challenge ahead. I need prayer."

—Beth Moore

"I have been driven many times upon my knees by the overwhelming conviction that I had nowhere else to go."

—Abraham Lincoln

RULE #7

The Queen Must Wake Up! Pray Up! And Crown Up!
You have to wake up feeling Queenish!

"O God, thou art my God; early will I seek thee..."

—Psalm 63:1

"A Queen is a woman who has MASTERED Herself. She's not perfect, but she is complete. She has come to the full realization that everything she needs to fulfill her mission can be found within. She's uncovered her powers and she knows how to use them. She's no longer on the path, she has BECOME the path."

—Author Unknown

RULE #8

The Queen Remains Focused on Her Faith, Family, and Future

"'For I know the plans I have for you,' declares the Lord, 'plans to prosper you and not to harm you, plans to give you hope and a future.'"

—Jeremiah 29:11

"Life is filled with external stimuli—look at this, read this, watch this, do this... we must train ourselves to focus on what's really important—our faith, our family, and our future. Understand, the ability to focus does not come naturally, it is a learned behavior. We must know our calling and go about fulfilling that calling every day. A focused mind allows us to move through life purposefully driven by the hand of God."

—Marva Dew

RULE #9

Steady MUST Be the Head That Wears the Crown

"Let your eyes look straight ahead; fix your gaze directly before you. Give careful thought to the paths for your feet and be steadfast in all your ways."

—Proverb 4:25, 26

"A double minded man is unstable in all his ways."

—James 1:8

"Never bend your head. Always hold it high. Look the world straight in the eye."

—Helen Keller

"What renders us unsteady is not life's constant demands, it is our inability to Manage life's constant demands. We must control our own selves. We must know who we are— our strengths and our weaknesses. We must take a long, sober, honest look at our own selves. And we must then set about conquering our weaknesses and controlling our short- comings. If you believe you have none then turn on the light, your eyes have become accustomed to walking in darkness."

—Marva Dew

"There's going to be very painful moments in your life that will change your entire world in a matter of minutes. These moments will change you. Let them make you stronger, smarter, and kinder. But don't you go and become someone that you're not. Cry. Scream if you have to. Then you straighten out that crown and keep on moving."

—Author Unknown

RULE #10

The Queen Knows Queenship Is Serious Business!
Humble I must stay. Hard I must work.

"I must work the works of Him that sent me, while it is day: the night cometh, when no man can work."

—John 9:4

"You can't smoke with them, drink with them, cuss with them, gossip with them, sex them, and then expect them to take your ministry seriously."

-Author Unknown

"We need women who are so strong they can be gentle, so educated they can be humble, so fierce they can be compassionate, so passionate they can be rational, and so disciplined they can be free."

—Kavita Ramdas

"God's work is serious business. I work hard for Him on purpose. Sweat makes my crown shine not tarnish."

—Marva Dew

RULE #11

Believing You Are Queen Is Not Enough... Most Often, You Must Set About Proving It

"You don't have to disrespect and insult others simply to hold your own ground. If you do, that shows how shaky your own position is."

—Red Haircrow

"When it comes to Queening, I can show you better than I can tell you! You can't just be a Queen in your own head. Your Queenship must come from the heart."

—Marva Dew

RULE #12

The Queen Works Faithfully For the Good of Others; the Growth of the Church; and the Glory of God

"He who began a good work in you will be faithful to complete it."

—Philippians 1:6

"The purpose of life is not to be happy. It is to be useful, to be honorable, to be compassionate, to have it make some difference that you have lived and lived well."

—Ralph Waldo Emerson

"God will not position you for greatness without preparing you for the position He assigned to you, to fulfill the promise He purposed for you."

—Author Unknown

RULE #13

The Queen is a Woman of Graceful Strength

"But He said to me, 'My grace is sufficient for you, for My power is made perfect in weakness.' Therefore I will boast all the more gladly about my weaknesses, so that Christ's power may rest on me."

—2nd Corinthians 12:9

"I will hold myself to a standard of grace not perfection."

—Emily Ley

"She made broken look beautiful and strong look invincible. She walked with the universe on her shoulders and made it look like a pair of wings."

—Ariana Dancu

RULE #14

The Queen is Confident —
Say it Loud, I'm the Queen & I'm Proud!

"My soul shall make her boast in the Lord: the humble shall hear thereof, and be glad..."

—Psalm 34:2

"Don't stop until you no longer have to introduce yourself. Don't stop until you're proud of yourself for doing or accomplishing whatever is set before you. Reverential pride adds value and brings about good. Selfish Pride is self-serving and brings about destruction. Don't stop until you know the difference."

—Marva Dew

"There is nothing more attractive than a woman who carries herself like a Queen and wears her confidence like a crown! Royalty or not, dignity and respect are every woman's birthright!"

—Khari Touré

"So I like what I see when I'm looking at me when I'm walking past the mirror. Ain't worried about you and what you gonna do, I'm a lady so I must stay classy..."

—"Just Fine" song by Mary J. Blige

RULE #15

The Queen is Not New to This — She's True to This

"But you, keep your head in all situations, endure hardship, do the work of an evangelist, discharge all the duties of your ministry."

—2nd Timothy 4:5

"Commitment means staying loyal to what you said you were going to do long after the mood you said it in has left."

—Author Unknown

RULE #16

There is No Match For a Queen with a Purpose and a Plan

"…She said to herself, 'If I might only touch the hem of His garment, I will be healed.'"

—Matthew 9:21

"God has a plan for your life. The enemy has a plan for your life. Be ready for both. Just be wise enough to know which one to battle and which one to embrace."

—Author Unknown

"If you don't sacrifice for what you want, then what you want might very well become the sacrifice. Stay on course. Fulfill your purpose."

—Author Unknown

"Pursue the things you love doing. And then do them so well that people can't take their eyes off you."

—Maya Angelou

RULE #17

The Queen Must Persevere, Persist & Press 100% of the Time

"...let us throw off everything that hinders and the sin that so easily entangles. And let us run with perseverance the race marked out for us."

—Hebrews 12:1

"The question isn't who is going to let me; it's who is going to stop me."

—Author Unknown

The enemy can't take you out so he's trying to wear you out. Push through to VICTORY!"

-Author Unknown

RULE #18

The Queen's Attitude
Can Make or Break Her Calling
It Must Be Aligned, Adjusted and Readjusted
on a Regular Basis

"Blind Pharisee! First clean the inside of the cup and dish, and then the outside also will be clean."

—Matthew 23:26

"Instead of obsessing over the things you can't change, focus on what you can change: your attitude, mindset, and energy."

—Author Unknown

"A bad attitude might be the result of unresolved issues that need to be dealt with and resolved lest those issues negatively and unknowingly impact your entire life."

—Sandra Ceaser

"A positive attitude is essential in life. It sets the pace for your day and flows from a humble yet grateful heart. A bad attitude is an affront to God. It flows from a prideful heart and can block love, friends, blessings, and destiny from finding you. Make the choice to control your attitude. Don't YOU be the reason YOU don't succeed."

—Marva Dew

"Queens: High heels, high standards, and high expectations. Smelling good, looking good, feeling good—highly ambitious, highly motivated, highly abundant, and in high demand—blessed, loved, and grateful."

—Author Unknown

RULE #19

The Queen Will Allow Her Smile to Change People, But She Will Not Allow People to Change Her Smile

"She is clothed with strength and dignity; she can laugh at the days to come."

—Proverb 3:5-6

"Sometimes I just look up, smile, and say, 'I know that was you God. Thanks.'"

—Author Unknown

"It was always the power of love that pulled us through, and it was the power of laughter that kept us from falling apart."

—Steve Rizzo

"I use my smile as a weapon of mass destruction. A single smile can help turn even the worst situations around."

—Marva Dew

RULE #20

The Queen Sets a Watch Over What She Hears, Sees, and Talks About

"It's not what you say to everyone else that determines your life. It's what you whisper to yourself that has the greatest power."

—Mark Hack

Until a person finds healing from their wounds and insecurities, they will be toxic or a burden to every person they run into."

—Author Unknown

"Be steady and well-ordered in your life so that you can be fierce and original in your work."

—Gustave Flaubert

"We must take seriously those things we purposefully set our gaze upon, listen to, and talk about. Those things become a part of who we are. We are sowing seeds into our own selves—our own lives, and the harvest is imminent. We must look for and listen for God in everything. Our speech should be such that God Himself would be able and willing to finish our sentences. We MUST set a watch over our own selves."

—Marva Dew

RULE #21

The Queen Knows How to Face Forward and Fall Back at the Same Time

"To everything there is a season, and a time to every purpose under the heaven: A time to be born, and a time to die; A time to plant, and a time to pluck up that which is planted; A time to kill, and a time to heal; A time to break down, and a time to build up; A time to weep, and a time to laugh; A time to mourn, and a time to dance; A time to cast away stones, and a time to gather stones together; A time to embrace, and a time to refrain from embracing; A time to get, and a time to lose; A time to keep, and a time to cast away; A time to rend, and a time to sew; A time to keep silence, and a time to speak; A time to love, and a time to hate; A time of war, and a time of peace."

—Ecclesiastes 3:1-8

"Sometimes you gotta fall back to get a better view."

—Author Unknown

"One's ability to face forward and fall back has to do with your willingness to simultaneously lead and follow. There comes a time when the best leaders, those with the ability to get the job done, must fall back—take the second seat—sit and settle while others lead. Facing Forward means remaining focused and ready to move, help, serve, or do what must

be done at a moment's notice. Falling Back requires a spirit of humility. It's knowing you could do the job, and most often do it better, but allowing others to lead or shine. Remember Queen, you will not always be the center of attention. Your way is not always the best way. Your voice is not always the final voice to be heard. Master the art of Facing Forward & Falling Back and you will be ready for every situation and every season of life."

—Marva Dew

RULE #22

The Queen's Integrity is Paramount!
It is on display at all times.
It speaks when she is silent.
It has the power to Build or Break.

"Whoever walks in integrity walks securely, but whoever takes crooked paths will be found out."

—Proverb 10:9

"Feel free to question my choice in clothes, my vote, or my opinion, but never question my integrity because my integrity is based on my calling, my purpose, and my right standing with God. A woman of integrity—there is no greater compliment; a woman of no integrity—no greater insult."

—Marva Dew

"Integrity is doing the right thing, even when no one is watching."

—C. S. Lewis

"You should be upright by yourself, not kept upright by those around you."

—Author Unknown

"There is no better test for a man's [woman's] integrity than his [her] behavior when he [she] is wrong."

—Marvin Williams

"We learned about honesty and integrity—that the truth matters... and success doesn't count unless you earn it fair and square."

—Michelle Obama

"No one will question your integrity if your integrity is not questionable."

—Nathaniel Bonner Jr.

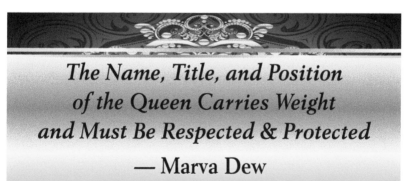

The Name, Title, and Position of the Queen Carries Weight and Must Be Respected & Protected

— Marva Dew

RULE #23

If the Crown Fits, Wear It
If It Doesn't, Add More Stones

"For this very reason, make every effort to add to your faith goodness; and to goodness, knowledge; and to knowledge, self-control; and to self-control, perseverance; and to perseverance, godliness; and to godliness, mutual affection; and to mutual affection, love. For if you possess these qualities in increasing measure, they will keep you from being ineffective and unproductive in your knowledge of our Lord Jesus Christ."

—2nd Peter 1:5-8

"You shouldn't want to be better than everyone else; you should want to be better than you ever were."

—Kay Wilson

"Never stop progressing in life. There will always be something that can and will make you better, sharper, smarter, and deeper. Read better books; learn another skill; take up a hobby... do something, anything to add value to your life. Continue to transform yourself, your life, and your mind. Make excellence your non-negotiable benchmark. Tomorrow's you must be better than today's."

—Marva Dew

"A self that goes on changing is a self that goes on living."

—Virginia Woolf

"All highly competent people continually search for ways to keep learning, growing, and improving. They do that by asking WHY. After all, the person who knows HOW will always have a job, but the person who knows WHY will always be the boss."

—Benjamin Franklin

RULE #24

The Queen Understands the Importance of Silence and Solitude

"But the Lord is in His holy temple: let all the earth keep silence before Him."

—Habakkuk 2:20

"And He said to them, 'Come aside by yourselves to a deserted place and rest a while.'"

—Mark 6:31

"The quieter you become, the more you can SEE."

—Marva Dew

"In the quiet, in the stillness, I know that You are God. In the secret of Your presence I know there I am restored. When You call I won't refuse. Each new day again I'll choose."

—Author Unknown

"You come home, make some tea, sit down in your armchair, and all around there's silence. Everyone decides for themselves whether that's loneliness or freedom."

—Author Unknown

RULE #25

Always Wear Your Invisible Crown!...
And if Necessary Wear a Real One

"She held her head high, imagining a crown upon it. And she vowed to look closely to notice the crown on the heads of other women she met today, too. She would acknowledge them all with a secret Queen smile."

—Author Unknown

"Walk in like a Queen with power and authority and you'll be treated as such. It's not smoke and mirrors, it's God's anointing."

—Marva Dew

RULE #26

The Queen Always Keeps Her Head Up— Even if She Has to Prop It Up

"Keep your head up, your eyes straight ahead, and your focus fixed on what is in front of you."

—Proverb 4:25

"Grow from the dirt they left you in."

—Author Unknown

"Keep your head UP in Failure and your head DOWN in Success."

—Author Unknown

"She has been through hell. So believe me when I say, fear her when she looks into a fire and smiles."

—Author Unknown

"She's a butterfly with a broken wing and bleeding feathers, but still she flies... but still, she flies..."

—J. Iron Word

"See how far you've come? Be proud of yourself. If nothing else, one day you can look someone straight in the eyes and say: 'But I lived through it, and it made me who I am today.'"

—Author Unknown

The Queen Knows How to Handle Her Business Without Letting People Know Her Business or Allowing Her Business to Handle Her

"Lions don't have to roar. There is power in silence, confidence, and persistence. Those who work don't talk, and those who talk don't work. Handle your business. Measure your efforts by results. Focus your time, energy, and activity on mastering and executing a plan."

—Les Brown

"A Queen knows how to build her empire with the same stones that were thrown at her."

—Author Unknown

The Queen Knows Her Money Matters

"The love of money is the root of all evil."

—1st Timothy 6:10

"Don't try to hang your hat where your hand can't reach."

—Mary Montoute

"There is no dignity quite so impressive, and no independence quite so important as living within your means."

—Calvin Coolidge

"Get out of debt as fast as you can, and keep out of debt, for that is the way in which the promise of God will be fulfilled to the people of His church, that they will become the richest of all people in the world."

—Joseph Fielding Smith

"A man is not a financial plan!"

—Kim Kiyosaki

"Queens, our money matters! We must learn to use money without allowing money to use us. And we must immediately cease from using money to impress others. Driving an expensive car means nothing if you have to borrow from others to pay the note or buy the gas. Financial debt is a tight noose that only the knowledge of money can free you from. We must learn to make money; save money; invest money; so that we are able to live comfortably (within our means) and have something to leave behind. We must prepare now for our present and our future. And we must teach those coming behind us the proper use and application of money. The first step to financial freedom is to trust God and His plan. Will a man rob God? We must tithe AND give offerings. Give God what belongs to Him (the 10% tithe and offerings) and watch God bless and increase the remainder. True financial freedom begins with God and ends with blessings.

—Marva Dew

RULE #29

The Queen's Beauty is an Asset Not a Requirement

"*Charm is deceptive, and beauty is fleeting; but a woman who fears the LORD is to be praised.*"

—Proverb 31:30

"*I'm not the average girl from your video and I ain't built like a supermodel, but I learned to love myself unconditionally because I Am A Queen.*"

—India Arie

"*You can't eat beauty. It doesn't sustain you. What is fundamentally beautiful is compassion, for yourself and those around you. That kind of beauty enflames the heart and enchants the soul.*"

—Lupita Nyong'o

"*A beautiful woman is a beautiful woman, but a beautiful woman with a brain—now that's a lethal combination.*"

—Prabal Gurung

"*Every woman is beautiful; she simply has to get to the point in life where she no longer needs a mirror to see it.*"

—Marva Dew

"Pretty Ugly—that's what you are if you're pretty on the outside and ugly on the inside. What's on the inside will soon distort what's on the outside and makeup, no matter how well applied, can't cover up a decaying spirit."

—Margaret Ceaser

"She was beautiful, but not like those girls in the magazines. She was beautiful, for the way she thought. She was beautiful, for the sparkle in her eyes when she talked about something she loved. She was beautiful, for her ability to make other people smile, even if she was sad. No, she wasn't beautiful for something as temporary as her looks. She was beautiful, deep down to her soul."

—F. Scott Fitzgerald

RULE #30

Everybody Wants to Be Queen but Few Can Stand the Weight of the Crown

"Uneasy lies the head that wears a crown."

—William Shakespeare

"Must Jesus bear the cross alone, and all the world go free? No; there's a cross for ev'ry one, and there's a cross for me. The consecrated cross I'll bear till death shall set me free,

and then go home my crown to wear, for there's a crown for
me."

—"Must Jesus Bear the Cross Alone?"
song by Thomas Shepherd

"The thing is to rely on God. The time will come when you
will regard all this misery as a small price to pay for having
been brought to that dependence. Meanwhile, the reality is
that relying on God has to begin all over again every day as
if nothing has yet been done."

—C. S. Lewis

"There are times in life and ministry when the weight of
our calling will cause us to bow and bend. It is in those
critical times that we must remember to shoulder our cross
and move forward in faith. The joy of the Lord must be our
strength—that which will cause us to rise yet again and give
it another try. Despite the weight, the cross we each bear
must make its way to Calvary."

—Marva Dew

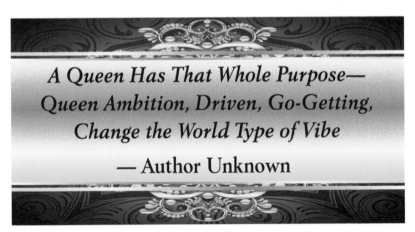

A Queen Has That Whole Purpose—
Queen Ambition, Driven, Go-Getting,
Change the World Type of Vibe

— Author Unknown

RULE #31

The Queen Can & Must Be Trusted—
Not Because of Who She Is,
But Because of Whom She Trusts

"Trust in the Lord with all thine heart; and lean not unto thine own understanding. In all thy ways acknowledge Him, and He shall direct thy paths."

—Proverb 3:5-6

"Trust is earned when actions meet words."

—Chris Butler

RULE #32

The Queen Knows Her Worth and Will
Not Entertain Bargain Shoppers!

"Who can find a virtuous woman? For her price is far above rubies."

—Proverb 31:10

"The moment you feel like you have to prove your worth to someone is the moment to absolutely and utterly walk away."

—Alysia Harris

"You can't act like flip flops and expect to be treated like Louboutins."

—Author Unknown

"Know your worth. It makes no sense to be second in someone's life, when you know you're good enough to be first in someone else's."

—Author Unknown

"Every woman should know this simple truth, You Are Already Enough."

—Marva Dew

RULE #33

A Queen By Any Other Name Is Still a Queen

"...Fear not, for I have redeemed thee; I have called thee by thy name; thou art Mine."

—Isaiah 43:1

"No matter what they call us, however they attack, no matter where they take us, we'll find our own way back."

—Andrew Lloyd Webber

"Whether you recognize it or not, I Am A Queen—not by default but by design."

—Marva Dew

"Never let anyone treat you like a yellow starburst. You are a pink starburst!"

—Author Unknown

"It's not what they call you it's what you answer to that matters."

—Author Unknown

RULE #34

Sometimes the Queen Has to Put on Her Big Girl Boots and Handle It

"Your Word is a lamp to guide my feet and a light for my path."

—Psalm 119:105

"If you're not prepared to go all the way, don't put your boots on in the first place."

—Edward Norton

"Don't start nothing, won't be nothing! It's just that simple."

—Yolanda Faye Ross

"The Bible does speak of the laying on of hands... and sometimes you just have to pull your hair back into a ponytail, grease your face, turn up the music, lace up your boots, and show a monkey she/he JUST climbed the wrong tree on the wrong day!... All for the greater cause, of course."

—Alicia Shorter

RULE #35

The Queen is Aware of Her Call to Lead

She leads by Precept and Example; She models the expected behavior at all times

"Likewise, tell the older women to be reverent in behavior, not to be slanderers or slaves to drink; they are to teach what is good, so that they may encourage the young women to love their husbands, to love their children, to be self-controlled, chaste, good managers of the household, kind, being submissive to their husbands, so that the word of God may not be discredited."

—Titus 2:3-5

"A good teacher/leader is like a candle—it consumes itself to light the way for others."

—Mustafa Ataturk

RULE #36

The Queen Knows How to Master the Art of Just Being

"But by the grace of God I am what I am, and His grace to me was not without effect."

—1st Corinthians 15:10a

"To be yourself in a world that is constantly trying to make you something else is the greatest accomplishment."

—Ralph Waldo Emerson

"There are days when I rise early, sit in front of a mirror, and complete my things-to-do list: Inhale. Exhale. Repeat. Go Back To Bed. The mirror is important because it reminds me to focus on ME—and that's enough for today."

—Marva Dew

RULE #37

The Queen is a Woman of Vision

"And the LORD answered me: 'Write the vision; make it plain on tablets, so he may run who reads it.'"

—Habakkuk 2:2

"Vision is not enough. It must be combined with venture. It is not enough to stare up the steps; we must step up the stairs."

—Vaclav Havel

"Vision is the source and hope of life. The greatest gift ever given to mankind is not the gift of sight, but the gift of vision. Sight is a function of the eyes; vision is a function of the heart. Eyes that look are common, but eyes that see are

rare. Nothing noble or noteworthy on earth was ever done without vision."
—Dr. Myles Munroe

"If you are working on something exciting that you really care about, you don't have to be pushed. The vision pulls you."
—Steve Jobs

"Vision without action is a daydream. Action without vision is a nightmare."
—Japanese Proverb

"People buy into the leader before they buy into the vision... If your vision doesn't cost you something, it's a daydream."
—John Maxwell

Sight is what you see with your eyes, vision is what you see with your mind."
—Robert Kiyosaki

"Vision is a divinely inspired mental picture of a preferable future. In these critical times, God's clarion call to leaders must be heard and moved upon. God is calling for visionary leaders with future-focused leadership. We must be willing to accept the call and meet the challenges of leadership. We must reach beyond where we are today and boldly embrace the vision and future God is calling us to."
—Dr. Gerald M. Dew

RULE #38

The Queen Sets and Maintains Healthy Personal Boundaries

"One of the most vital components to creating a happy, healthy and fulfilling relationship is to become a master at setting boundaries. Boundaries are what set the space between where you end and the other person begins."

—Jennifer Twardowski

"The important thing is that boundaries be permeable enough to allow passing and strong enough to keep out danger."

—Author Unknown

"Boundaries need to be communicated, first verbally and then with action."

—Dr. Henry Cloud

"Healthy boundaries are not walls. They are the gates and fences that allow you to enjoy the beauty of your own garden."

—Lydia Hall

"Each time you set a healthy boundary you say 'yes' to more freedom."

—Nancy Levin

"Setting personal boundaries is extremely important and takes courage. It tells others where their stopping point is with you and it reminds you where your stopping point must be with others. Setting boundaries is not about keeping others out as much as it is about keeping you in and maintaining self. We teach others how to treat us by allowing ourselves to accept and/or tolerate certain things and behaviors. Setting boundaries is a form of love. Well defined boundaries convey three messages: (1) yes; (2) no; (3) that's far enough. Not everyone will understand or appreciate the need for your boundaries, but set and maintain them anyway—your life will be the richer—your Queendom will be fortified."

—Marva Dew

RULE #39

The Queen Protects Her Mind and Her Thinking

"...Whatever is true, whatever is honorable, whatever is just, whatever is pure, whatever is pleasing, whatever is commendable, if there is any excellence and if there is anything worthy of praise, think about these things."

—Philippians 4:8

"Your mind is a garden, your thoughts are the seeds, you can grow flowers or you can grow weeds."

—Author Unknown

"We cannot control the 1,000's of idle thoughts that cross our minds on a daily basis—they can and will pop up out of nowhere. We can, however, control the things we Think on and give our attention to. We must control our thinking. As a Queen thinketh in her heart, so is she."

—Marva Dew

RULE #40

Think Like a Queen

"Let this mind be in you which was also in Christ Jesus..."

—Philippians 2:5

"On challenging days or when faced with opposition, sometimes you have to remember who you are; remember whose you are; straighten your crown; and march on like the Queen you are!"

—Author Unknown

"Two things to remember in life: (1) Take care of your thoughts when you are alone; (2) Take care of your words when you are with people."

—Author Unknown

"First, Think. Second, Believe. Third, Dream. And finally, Dare."

—Walt Disney

RULE #41

The Queen Values Education

"The heart of the discerning acquires knowledge, for the ears of the wise seek it out."

—Proverb 18:15

"I don't mind if I have to sit on the floor at school. All I want is an education."

—Malala Yousufzai

"We educate women because it is smart. We educate women because it changes the world."

—Drew Faust

"Choose to be a life-long learner."

—Dr. Gerald Dew

RULE #42

The Queen is a Seeker of Wisdom, Knowledge, and Understanding

"For the Lord gives wisdom; from His mouth come knowledge and understanding."

—Proverb 2:6

"She speaks with wisdom, and faithful instruction is on her tongue."

—Proverb 31:26

"Not to know is bad. Not to wish to know is worse."

—African Proverb

"Wisdom is Godly insight and enlightenment. It is the ability to discern what is right or true. Wisdom begins and ends with the fear of God. It cannot be taught or gained through experience. Wisdom is a supernatural gift from God. It is impossible to have wisdom without Him."

—Marva Dew

RULE #43

The Queen is a Servant at Heart
She Works to Serve Not to Be Served

"Whoever wants to become great among you must be your servant, and whoever wants to be first must be your slave— just as the Son of Man did not come to be served, but to serve, and to give His life as a ransom for many."

—Matthew 20:26-28

"Work for a cause not for applause. Live your life to express not to impress. Don't strive to make your presence noticed just make your absence felt."

—Author Unknown

"At the end of our lives, we will not be judged by how many diplomas we have received, how much money we have made or how many great things we have done. We will be judged by, 'I was hungry and you gave me to eat. I was naked and you clothed me. I was homeless and you took me in.'"

—Mother Theresa

"While others are congratulating themselves, I have to sit humbly at the foot of the cross and marvel that I'm saved at all."

—C. H. Spurgeon

"One of the greatest things you can do to help others is not just to share and give what you have, but to help them discover what they have within themselves to help others."

—Rita Zahara

"The Lord has from the beginning of time provided ways for His disciples to help. He has invited His children to consecrate their time, their means, and themselves to join with Him in serving others. He has invited and commanded us to participate in His work to lift up those in need."

—Henry Eyring

RULE #44

The Queen Knows How to
Roll Up Her Sleeves & Get the Job DONE

"As long as it is day, we must do the works of Him who sent me. Night is coming, when no one can work."

—John 9:4

"On your best day, in your finest hour, the most you can ever hope to be is a servant for our Lord and Savior Jesus Christ. So do the work—the hard work, the thankless work, the good work. Rest is on the other side of the river."

—Marva Dew

"The best job goes to the person who can get it done without passing the buck or coming back with excuses."

—Napoleon Hill

"If you're not willing to work hard for it, don't complain about not having it."

—Author Unknown

"Work hard in silence—let success make the noise."

—Author Unknown

#Queen—Her hustle is tough, and her swag, outstanding. Most are distracted by her pretty face, but a real Queen can hold her own and then some. She knows how to handle her business. Experiences have taught her who to keep in her court, and while she may seem to be too much for a Joker, she's perfect for a King.

—Author Unknown

RULE #45

The Queen Never Leaves Her Throne to Address Peasants Throwing Stones

"And I sent messengers unto them, saying, 'I am doing a great work, so that I cannot come down: why should the work cease, whilst I leave it, and come down to you?'"

—Nehemiah 6:3

"Maintain your position in spite of opposition."

—Darlene Collazo

"There will be haters. Your haters will see you walk on water and say it's because you can't swim."

—Author Unknown

"The lion doesn't lose sleep over the opinions of sheep."

—Author Unknown

"Sometimes you have to let the trash take itself out."

—Author Unknown

RULE #46

There Will Be Times When the Crown Gets Heavy, Tight, and Hard to Wear... But Wear It

"We are hard pressed on every side, but not crushed; perplexed, but not in despair; persecuted, but not abandoned; struck down, but not destroyed."

—2nd Corinthians 4:8, 9

"Strong women don't play victim, don't make themselves look pitiful, and don't point fingers. They stand and they deal."

—Mandy Hale

RULE #47

You Can't Put a Crown on a Clown and Expect a Queen

"A foolish woman is clamorous: she is simple, and knoweth nothing."

—Proverb 9:13

"Entertain a clown and you become a part of the circus."

—Author Unknown

"A foolish girl will PLAY hard to GET. A wise woman will BE hard to FORGET."

—Author Unknown

"If you act like a clown, people will expect you to entertain them. The Queen must have character not be a character. People will laugh with you and will then turn right around and laugh at you and about you. If you want to be taken seriously—stand for something. Find at least one honorable thing to stand for—one cause you are willing to give your life for and to… find that thing and then work with everything

within you to bring it to pass with a spirit of excellence. And watch that same laughter from others, turn to amazed awe."

—Marva Dew

RULE #48

The Queen Understands Three Indisputable Facts:

1. You Cannot Teach What You Do Not Know
2. You Cannot Lead Where You Will Not Go
3. They Will Not Learn What You Do Not Show

RULE #49

The Queen Knows How to Make Her Presence Known and Her Absence Felt

"Knowing when to walk away is WISDOM. Being able to is COURAGE. Walking away with your head held high is DIGNITY."

—Author Unknown

"There's a trick to the graceful exit. It begins with the vision to recognize when a job, a life stage, or a relationship is over—and let it go. It means leaving what's over without denying its validity or past importance in our lives. It

involves a sense of future, a belief that every exit line is an entry—that we are moving up, rather than out."

—Ellen Goodman

RULE #50

The Queen Knows When to Let Her Silence Speak for Her

"Even fools are thought wise if they keep silent, and discerning if they hold their tongues."

—Proverb 17:28

"Sometimes, not saying anything is the best answer. Silence can never be misquoted."

—Author Unknown

"When a woman stops talking to you, listen to what she says with her eyes."

—Victor Hugo

"Don't mistake silence for weakness. Smart people don't plan big moves out loud."

—Author Unknown

"Preach the gospel every day; and if necessary, use words."

—St. Francis of Assisi

RULE #51

The Queen Understands Her Gifts Will Make Room for Her

"A man's gift makes room for him, and brings him before great men."

—Proverb 18:16

"The meaning of life is to find your gift. The purpose of life is to give it away."

—Pablo Picasso

"One of the Queen's finest treasures and greatest gifts are her pearls of wisdom. They are tried and true. Receive them & you will go far use them & you will go farther."

—Rose Johnson

"Don't make the mistake of becoming too cute, too comfortable, or too common with God and His gifts. We are not called by God to sit and see. We are gifted by God to do the work of God. Identify your spiritual gift/s; use them to build and strengthen the body of Christ; to win the lost and make disciples. We must use God's gifts to build God's kingdom."

—Marva Dew

"Everyone has their own path. Walk yours with integrity and wish all others peace on their journey. When your paths merge, rejoice for their presence in your life. When the paths are separated, return to the wholeness of yourself, give thanks for the footprints left on your soul, and embrace the time to journey on your own."

—Author Unknown

RULE #52

The Queen Stands Ready to Lead

"A true leader has the confidence to stand alone, the courage to make tough decisions, and the compassion to listen to the needs of others. He does not set out to be a leader, but becomes one by the equality of his actions and the integrity of his intent."

—Douglas MacArthur

"The most powerful leadership tool you have is your own personal example."

—John Wooden

"Leadership is about making others BETTER as a result of your presence and making SURE that impact lasts in your ABSENCE."

—Author Unknown

RULE #53

The Queen is Strategic in Her Thinking

"The essence of strategy is choosing what not to do."

—Mikhael Porter

"Quiet the mind and the soul will speak."

—Majaya Bhagavati

"Strategic thinking is both creative and critical. We must never stop thinking, wondering, and discovering new and innovative ideas and concepts. We must purposefully train our minds to look at something/anything/everything from every angle. Focus on what is absolutely necessary IN the moment and FOR the future."

—Marva Dew

"To the Jews I became as a Jew, in order to win Jews. To those under the law I became as one under the law (though I myself am not under the law) so that I might win those under the law. To those outside the law I became as one outside the law (though I am not free from God's law but am under Christ's law) so that I might win those outside the law. To the weak I became weak, so that I might win the weak. I have become all things to all people that I might by all means save some. I do it all for the sake of the gospel, so that I may share in its blessings."

—1ˢᵗ Corinthians 9:20-23

RULE #54

The Queen Has Keen Intuition, but Knows it is the Holy Spirit Who Gives True Insight and Foresight

"The same power that raised Christ from the dead is inside of you."

—Romans 8:11

"Never underestimate the power of a woman's intuition. Some women can recognize Game before you even play it."

—Author Unknown

RULE #55

The Queen Lives a Life OF Purpose ON Purpose — Her Life Is Intentional

"Do you know that nothing you do in this life will ever matter, unless it is about loving God and loving the people He has made."

—Francis Chan

"A woman who walks in purpose doesn't have to chase people or opportunities. Her light causes people and opportunities to pursue her."

—Author Unknown

"Your talk talks and your walk talks, but your walk talks louder than your talk talks."

—John Maxwell

"Some people influence the masses… some influence the people that influence the masses."

—Author Unknown

"When it comes to life, use Faith, Finesse, and downright Fierceness to accomplish your goals and drive you forward."

—Marva Dew

RULE #56

The Queen Knows How to Keep It:
Real • Relevant • Responsible •
Righteous • Revolutionary

RULE #57

The Queen Knows How To Be Herself—Unapologetically
She is Aware of Her Shortcomings and Flaws and Comfortable in Her Perfect Imperfection

"But by the grace of God I am what I am, and His grace to me was not without effect."

—1st Corinthians 15:10

"At the end of the day, I'm a good woman. I'm not perfect by any means but my intentions are good, my heart is pure and I love hard with everything I've got and because of those things... I'm worth it. Always have been and always will be."

—Author Unknown

"No one is you and that is your Super Power."

—Elyse Santilli

RULE #58

Inside Every Queen Beats the Heart of a Warrior

"Wherefore take unto you the whole armour of God, that ye may be able to withstand in the evil day, and having done all, to stand."

—Ephesians 6:13

"The supreme challenge of a warrior is to turn an enemy's fearful wrath into harmless laughter."

—Morihei Ueshiba

"She will rise! With a spine of steel and a roar like thunder! She will rise!"

—Nicole Lyons

"She has the mindset of a Queen and the heart of a warrior. She is everything all at once and too much for anyone who doesn't deserve her. She Is You! She Is Me! She Is Us!"

—Author Unknown

"And then one day, I discovered by own light, my own inner-gangster. I snatched my power back and the game changed."

—Author Unknown

*"She is sweet, loving, kind, and gentle, but don't be fooled—
she is a Warrior Queen! She is not lost in the fight and fire—
she is built for it!"*

—Author Unknown

*"A warrior is not only the woman who goes out and conquers
the enemy on the battlefield. She is also the woman who gets
up each morning, readies herself and her family, goes to work,
cooks and cleans. She is the wife, the mother, the student, the
chef, and the chauffeur. And she is a warrior because she does
all this knowing full well tomorrow awaits her."*

—Marva Dew

RULE #59

Dust Settles, Queens Don't

*"I don't play disrespect. I don't play dishonesty. I don't play
disloyal. And I don't play sticking around to see whether
or not you want to learn how to be any of the above. If it's
not already present, I'm already a thing of the past. I won't
settle for less than I deserve. Call it what you want. I call it
standards."*

—Catherine Simpson

*"Don't settle. Either they will wake up to the fact that you
are worth more... or you will."*

—Charles Orlando

"There came a time in my life when certain things became non-negotiable: (1) I only ride in the backseat if I'm in a limo; (2) If I'm eating steak its filet mignon; (3) When I enter a room, the molecular structure of that room must change in order to accommodate not my pride, but my position. I am a woman of God- His representative. I Do Not Settle! And that's not bragging, that's a statement of facts."

—Marva Dew

RULE #60

The Queen Knows How and When to Go Back to the Motherland...

That Place Where It All Began,
That Place Where It All Made Sense

The Queen May Leave the Room or Yield the Floor, But She Never Relinquishes the Throne!

— Marva Dew

RULE #61

The Queen Cannot Be Denied and She Will Not Stop
Her Direction is Always Forward!

"Therefore, my beloved brethren, be ye steadfast, unmoveable, always abounding in the work of the Lord, forasmuch as ye know that your labour is not in vain in the Lord."

—1st Corinthians 15:58

"Only God knows the future. Therefore, the Queen must remain in a perpetual state of readiness. She doesn't get ready... She Stays Ready!"

—Marva Dew

"Queens are on a focused mission to uplift our Kings; raise powerful, intelligent children; erase the myth that Sister-Queens can't get along; and crush society's one sided view of beauty—all while elevating the standards and eliminating distractions."

—Author Unknown

"Life itself will at times present what appear to be mountains before you. In order to get to the other side of them you don't necessarily need a trained mountain climber, sometimes you just need someone familiar with breaking rocks."

—Marva Dew

"Some quit due to slow progress, never grasping the fact that slow progress IS progress."

—Author Unknown

"Don't stumble over something behind you."

—Author Unknown

"Let us strive to improve ourselves, for we cannot remain stationary; one either progresses or retrogrades."

—Marie Du Deffand

RULE #62

When the Queen Speaks, She Must Have Something to Say—Her Words Matter

"She openeth her mouth with wisdom; and in her tongue is the law of kindness."

—Proverb 31:26

"Wisdom is knowing when to speak your mind and when to mind your speech."

—Kamari Lyrikal

"For having expressed an opinion, however far-fetched, we straightway become its slave, ready to die defending it, and even ready to believe it. And many continue to be martyrs

to causes which have ceased to exist, their crowns rusting upon their heads as tin wreaths rust upon forgotten tombs."

—Paul Eldridge

"Taste your words before you spit them out."

—Author Unknown

"Speak the truth even if your voice shakes."

—Author Unknown

"Every single time we talk, give an opinion, answer a question, etc., we tell people who we are at our core. We must give prayerful, careful consideration to all things before we speak. And in this time of social media when text-talking is the norm, we must find a way to say only what is necessary lest our words be misinterpreted and our message distorted.

"What matters is not only what we say, but how we say it. An unknown writer said, 'A foolish man tells a woman to stop talking, but a wise man tells her that her mouth is extremely beautiful when her lips are closed.'

"We must master the art of purposeful communication—the ability to send the right Message, in the right Manner, at the right Moment, to the right people, for the right reason in a way in which it will be received and moved upon."

—Marva Dew

RULE #63

Queens Are Crowned with Glory and Honor
—Authority is Their Birthright

"When I look at Your heavens, the work of Your fingers, the moon and the stars that You have established; what are human beings that You are mindful of them, mortals that You care for them? Yet You have made them a little lower than God, and crowned them with glory and honor. You have given them dominion over the works of Your hands; You have put all things under their feet..."

—Psalm 8:3-6

"I walk in with God-given authority. Period."

—Marva Dew

"Though God hath raised me high, yet this I count the glory of my crown: that I have reigned with your loves. And though you have had, and may have many mightier and wiser princes sitting in this seat; yet you never had, nor shall have any that will love your better."

—Queen Elizabeth II

RULE #64

The Ear of the Queen Must Be Protected

"Listen to advice and accept discipline, and at the end you will be counted among the wise."

—Proverb 19:20

"Avoid head trash. Don't be a garbage can for anything that does not feed your intellect, stimulate your imagination, or make you a more compassionate peaceful person. Refuse to open your mind to other people's trash. Tune out anything that promotes conflict or controversy. This can infect you with a mind virus of cynicism or defeat, and you won't even know it!"

—Author Unknown

"Who gossips to you will gossip about you. And any dog that'll take a bone will bring a bone. Watch who you listen to because the same one who runs to tell you about others will run to tell others about you and what you said about them."

—Vera Mills

"Train yourself to listen to what is being said and what is not being said—both matter."

—Marva Dew

"Be careful what you say to yourself. You're listening."

—Steve Wentworth

RULE #65

The Queen's Liberation & Freedom is Dependent Upon Her Soul Power

"But you will receive power when the Holy Spirit has come upon you…"

—Acts 1:8

"If you see the Holy Spirit as a power, you will say, 'I want more of the Holy Spirit' (especially in time of need). But if you see Him more as a Person, you will say, 'I want the Holy Spirit to have more of me.'"

—Skip Heitzig

"Forget her looks. How about her insane work ethic, her unstoppable ambition and her ridiculously dope soul."

—Author Unknown

RULE #66

The Queen Will Never Allow Her CROWN to Become Bigger and/or More Important Than Her CALLING

"From everyone who has been given much, much will be demanded; and from the one who has been entrusted with much, much more will be asked."

—Luke 12:48

"It's not the size of the crown but the heart of the Queen that matters."

—Author Unknown

"This life is not about being the shining star of your own movie. It's about getting the Lord's work done—winning the lost and making disciples. This is a High Calling and a High Privilege...humble yourself and work!"

—Marva Dew

RULE #67

The Queen Leaves a Legacy:

Something that is handed down or remains from one generation to the next; a heritage; a tradition

"One generation commends Your works to another; they tell of Your mighty acts."

—Psalm 145:4

"Legacy is not leaving something for people. It's leaving something in people."

—Author Unknown

"Leave a spiritual legacy in your family, or you leave no legacy at all."

—Author Unknown

"The things you do for yourself are gone when you are gone, but the things you do for others remain as your legacy."

—Kalu Ndukwe Kalu

"I would like to be known as a caring woman; a woman of integrity; a woman of substance; a woman willing to fight the good fight; a woman of her word; a woman of truth; a woman of uncompromised values. I would like to be known as a lady—graceful strength personified; a teacher/leader— one who consistently modeled the expected behavior; one who made a positive impact on others. I want my Sister-Queens to say, 'She helped to bring out the best in me- whether she had to draw it out or drive it out.' I would like to be known as God's fierce warrior and humble servant. And I would like to leave the essence of who I am to/for others. Not in an attempt to duplicate myself, but my way of sharing the best of myself with another woman—another Queen.

"Ask yourself, after I'm gone, what will I be remembered for? If the answer is clothes, property, or money—then dig deeper. Leave something on the heart, the mind, and the soul. Leave a testimony; a scripture; a smile; or a lesson. Leave something that others can build upon. I will not live forever; therefore, I must leave something behind that will. Leaving a legacy is allowing someone else to stand on your shoulders and reach the next level without you being present. That's leaving a legacy!"

—Marva Dew

The Queen's Rules & Noble Directives

...Just Between Us Queens

RULE #68

The Queen Believes in the Power of SISTERHOOD

"Every sister will be a sister and every sister will have a sister; so that no sister will stand alone."

—Sisters For Sisters Bonding Conference
Marva Dew, Founder

"Christian sisterhood, in its purest form, is a SPIRITUAL FORCE of love, faith, and unity. It does not just happen. It must be developed, nurtured, and perfected. Sisterhood is a FORMIDABLE FORCE in and of itself. Its power cannot be denied and its strength cannot be measured. True sisterhood is an INTENSE FORCE—powerful, purposeful, and potent. Sisterhood: Iron Sharpening Iron!"

—Marva Dew

"Sisterhood—from the outside looking in, you can never understand it. From the inside looking out, you can never explain it."

—Author Unknown

"Individually we are a drop but together we are an ocean."

—Ryunosuke Satoro

"If you ever find yourself talking about another sister, make sure you finish off by saying, 'She's doing her thing though.'"

—Boss Chicks

"For my sister I am here. For my sister I am here. For my sister I will do anything. I am praying for her; I'm crying with her; I'll give her a song to sing—for my sister I will do anything..."

—"For My Sister I Am Here"
song by Yvonne Seabrooks

RULE #69

Queens Uplift Other Queens—Period

"We who are strong ought to bear with the failings of the weak and not to please ourselves. Each of us should please our neighbors for their good, to build them up."

—Romans 15:1

"You can tell who the strong women are. They are the ones you see building up one another instead of tearing each other down."

—Author Unknown

"Be a woman other women can trust. Have the courage to tell another woman direct when she has offended, hurt,

or disappointed you. Successful women have a loyal tribe of loyal and honest women behind them. Not haters. Not backstabbers or women who whisper behind their back. Be a woman who lifts other women."

—Sophia Nelson

"When the blind man carries the lame man, both go forward."

—Swedish Proverb

"Snowflakes are one of nature's most fragile things, but just look at what they can do when they stick together."

—Author Unknown

"Unity, to be real, must stand the severest strain without breaking."

—Mahatma Gandhi

"I Am My Sister's Keeper!" So often we make that declaration without giving careful and prayerful consideration to what we are signing up for. Keeping another sister is serious business, it requires us to encourage, teach, train, guide, and guard. We must be willing to watch and defend; correct and reprove. There is an unwritten, but well understood Sister Code we must adhere to. The good news is this, if we fail in our assignment, I AM—the great I AM—God Himself is the ultimate keeper. I AM my sister's keeper is both a testament and a praise report."

—Marva Dew

RULE #70

The Queen Lets Other Queens Know... Your Crown is Slipping

"Iron Sharpens Iron, so one man sharpens the countenance of his friend."

—Proverb 27:17

"Do not look where you fell, but where you slipped!"

—African Proverb

"Fix another Queen's crown without telling the world it's crooked."

—Author Unknown

"Although we aim for perfection, we have not yet obtained it. There will be times when our crown will slip—an off day, a bad decision, a slip of the tongue, etc. As Sister-Queens we must love one another enough to be honest with one another. To encourage my sister means telling her in love those things she does well; as well as telling her in love those things that are wrong and must be corrected. If my sister's crown is slipping, that means she's fallen short of God's mark or is off point. I am not her judge and she is not the sum total of her mistake. If I see her falter and I do nothing—I have in that moment fallen below her bottom line."

—Marva Dew

RULE #71

Queen… If You Can't Fix Your Crown, Fix Your Face

"Because the Sovereign Lord helps me, I will not be disgraced. Therefore have I set my face like flint, and I know I will not be put to shame."

—Isaiah 50:7

"I don't just listen to your words. I watch your face. I stare into your eyes. I check out your body language. I peep your tone. I make note of your use of words. I hear what you don't say. I interpret your silences."

—Author Unknown

RULE #72

The Queen Will Fight With, for and Alongside Other Queens Without Fear or Hesitation

"Fight the good fight of the faith. Take hold of the eternal life to which you were called when you made your good confession in the presence of many witnesses."

—1st Timothy 6:12

"When you see a good fight, get in it!"

—Nelson Ceaser

"First they ignore you, then they laugh at you, then they fight you, then you win."

—Mahatma Ghandi

"As long as we live, we fight, and as long as we are fighting, that is a sign that we are not defeated and that the good spirit dwells within us. And if death does not meet you as the victor, he should find you a warrior."

—St. Augustine

RULE #73

The Queen Doesn't Take Herself, Her Title, or the Crown Too Seriously— It's the Work That Matters

"Don't take yourself too seriously. Laugh a lot. Enjoy your time with family. Appreciate the unique talents of others. Trust in God. Love your neighbor. Say you're sorry. Forgive and work hard."

—Willie Robertson

"Careful you don't get drunk on your own sweet kool-aid."

—Marva Dew

RULE #74

Beware of Imposters: Drama Queens
Real Queens Don't Do Drama

"There comes a time in your life when you walk away from all the drama and the people who create it. You surround yourself with people who love you, challenge you, and make you laugh. Learn from the bad and focus on the good. Love the people who treat you right and pray for the ones who don't. Life is too short to be anything but happy. Falling down is part of life. Getting back up is living."

—Jose N. Harris

"A life filled with silly drama and gossip indicates that a person is disconnected from purpose and lacking meaningful goals. People on a path of purpose don't have time for drama."

—Brenda Burchard

"Look for a protégé not a parasite. A parasite looks for what's in your hand. A protégé looks for what's in your heart."

— Author Unknown

"Misery loves good company, so if you are surrounded with drama, gossip, and fools you may want to consider that you are presently at risk of becoming one of them."

—Bryant McGill

Queen Agenda

"I am a Queen. I represent Passion, Purpose and Positivity. I will spread love to my fellow Queen, encourage and support her. I know the power within me and I will use it to help uplift those around me. Queens recognize Queens, so I'm going to keep my crown on so that you can see that I am you and you are me."

—Saloan Rochelle

RULE #75

The Queen is Selective About Who Serves With and Alongside Her
Her Royal Court Often Appears Closed

"...So Esther's maids and her chamberlains came and told it her..."

—Esther 4:4

"A circle of women may be the most powerful force known to humanity. If you have one, embrace it. If you need one, seek it. If you find one, for the love of all that is good and holy, dive in; hold on; love it up."

—Author Unknown

"Call it a Clan; call it a Network; call it a Tribe; call it a Family: Whatever you call it, whoever you are, you need one."

—Jane Howard

"If you're the only one in your crew shining, you are not the boss, you are the target."

—Author Unknown

"You cannot win on a losing team; and all I do is WIN."

—Doniella Ligon

"I believe a Queen's Tribe should consist of:

- A Warrior (Fighter)
- A Wailer (Gentle Soul)
- A Worker (Ride Or Die Sistah')
- A Witness (Scout)
- A Worshipper (Rock)

The Bible says, 'Lay hands suddenly on no man (1st Timothy 5:22).' Queen, give careful, prayerful consideration to *who serves with and alongside you. A snake will coil around you and then look you right in the eye while it bites you."*

—Marva Dew

RULE #76

The Queen Knows There's Strength in Numbers

"Two are better than one, because they have a good return for their labor: if either of them falls down, one can help the other up. But pity anyone who falls and has no one to help them up. Also, if two lie down together, they will keep warm. But how can one keep warm alone? Though one may be over-powered, two can defend themselves. A cord of three strands is not quickly broken."

—Ecclesiastes 4:9-12

"If you mess with one sister, then there is always a crazy big sister and a crazier little sister that you don't want to deal with."

—Author Unknown

"My sisters are a force to be reckoned with. Together we are an impenetrable wall of strength, support, and solidarity. Trust me; you don't want to poke the sisterhood bear."

—Marva Dew

RULE #77

Queens Recognize Queens
They Don't Compete —They Compliment

"I plead with Euodia and I plead with Syntyche to be of the same mind in the Lord. Yes, and I ask you, my true companion, help these women since they have contended at my side in the cause of the gospel, along with Clement and the rest of my co-workers, whose names are in the book of life."

—Philippians 4:2-3

"I am not your enemy! I am your sister! Though we be separate, we are one! I see you because I am you."

—Marva Dew

RULE #78

The Queen Will Help to Meet the Needs of Other Queens

"Share with the Lord's people who are in need. Practice hospitality."

—Romans 12:13

"We are not here on earth to see through one another, we are here to see one another through."

—Author Unknown

"Queens have a relationship. We are Sisters. Helping one another is our mandate, our command. So often what prevents us from helping one another is the fear that someone else will do better, have more, or be more than we are. Sisterhood dictates and demands that we put the needs of others above our own selfish fears and desires. If I am elevated only because I'm standing on your back and illuminated because of your tears, then my position and power have been diminished to nothing at my own hand. My true strength lies in my willingness to raise my sister above my own self. To see her on a level that causes me to strain my neck is the true test of Authentic Sisterhood."

—Marva Dew

Be the kind of Woman/Queen that makes other women want to be you...then encourage them to Aim Higher...Much Higher! Draw them to you and then lead them to someone greater...lead them to God.

— Marva Dew

The Queen's
Rules &
Family Jewels

The Eyes of the Future Are Upon the Queen

"Train up a child in the way he should go and when he is old he will not depart from it."

—Proverb 22:6

"Tiny is her stature. Mighty is her roar. She is a lioness who will one day be in complete control of her kingdom. She is a princess—destined to be Queen!"

—Author Unknown

There's a Queen Inside Every Princess
Teach Her, Train Her, Try Her, Then Loose Her, and Let Her Go

"Your greatest contribution to the kingdom of God may not be something you do but someone you raise."

—Andy Stanley

"Princess, slay your own dragons."

—Author Unknown

"If you want children to keep their feet on the ground, put some responsibility on their shoulders."

—Abigail Van Buren

"Queens are developed over time not overnight—it's a process. Don't rush the process."

—Marva Dew

"Help people help themselves. Don't judge, just help. In this process, be cautious to simply point them in the right direction and help them get moving. Don't make your journey theirs, nor make their journey yours."

—Dr. Steve Maraboli

RULE #81

The Queen Never Stops Raising the Standards
(Queenship is Earned — Not Given)

"When I was a child, I talked like a child, I thought like a child, I reasoned like a child. When I became a man, I put the ways of childhood behind me."

—1st Corinthians 13:11

"If your job is to leaven ordinary lives with elevating spectacle, be elevating or be gone."

—George Will

"If we are serious about raising the standards for ourselves and others, Excellence must be our standard at all times; and Mediocrity our greatest fear."

—Marva Dew

"Don't go looking for a good person until you, yourself, have become a good person. You must meet the requirements of your requirements."

—Author Unknown

"If you sincerely want to change your life: raise your standards. What changes people is when their shoulds become musts."

—Tony Robbins

"Everybody wants to be a diamond, but very few are willing to get cut."

—Author Unknown

"Every woman should have standards that govern the way she lives her life. She must know her bottom line—the line that must not and will not be crossed—the line she will not fall below. Every woman must know those things she will and will not tolerate. Once you have your bottom line in place, you must grow from that point upwards. Continue to raise the standard for your life until you have reached a state of holiness that will bring a smile to the face of God. And having done so, hold up a banner for others to see, learn from, and follow."

—Marva Dew

RULE #82

The Queen is Keeper of Her Castle and Guardian of Her Queendom at All Times

"She looketh well to the ways of her household…"

—Proverb 31:27

"To Keep:

- *To Pay Attention To; Watch Over; Attend To*
- *To Defend Diligently; To Have Charge Over*
- *To Maintain; Take Care of*

Man is called to be the HEAD of the home. Woman is called to be the KEEPER of the home (not to be confused with called to be the housekeeper—although her duties certainly include chores and he should certainly assist). Both are important. Both are powerful. They are not interchangeable roles, but they must both work together for marital harmony. And know this—the charge to be a Keeper of the Home is not for married women only. Single sisters must learn to be keepers of their homes also."

—Marva Dew

"God bless you, my beloved sisters, who stand as the Queens in your home that you may be happy with that happiness

which comes of the knowledge that you are loved and honored and treasured."

—Gordon B. Hinckley

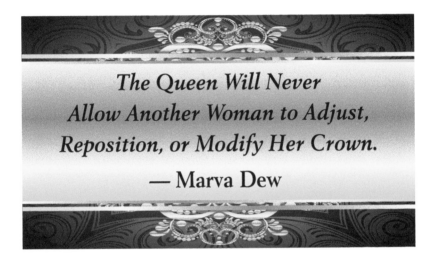

*The Queen Will Never
Allow Another Woman to Adjust,
Reposition, or Modify Her Crown.*

— Marva Dew

RULE #83

The Queen is at Peace
in Her Single Season

*"Be Alone. Eat alone, take yourself on dates, and sleep
alone. In the midst of this you will learn about yourself. You
will grow, you will figure out what inspires you, you will
curate your own dreams, your own beliefs, your own stun-
ning clarity, and when you do meet the person who makes
your cells dance, you will be sure of it, because you are sure
of yourself."*

—Bianca Sparacino

"If God is making you wait then be prepared to receive more than what you asked for."

—Author Unknown

"A woman sitting by herself is not waiting for you."

—Caitlin Stacey

"No matter how long you have been waiting, the man God has for you will surpass your expectations. You will meet him when God says so. Not a minute early, not a moment later."

—Michelle McKinney Harris

"Don't be a Queen looking for and waiting for the right king. Be a Queen busy being the right Queen—one who is busy building herself and her Queendom until her king arrives. And if he never arrives—that's his loss. Not every Queen requires or desires a king. Your Queen status stands! What is a Queen without a King? A QUEEN!"

—Marva Dew

"Your king won't show up until you remove the jokers."

—Author Unknown

"Be with someone who wants to chase God with you."

—Author Unknown

RULE #84

A King That Finds His Queen Finds a Good Thing and Obtains Favor

"The Lord God said, 'It is not good for the man to be alone. I will make a helper suitable for him.'"

—Genesis 2:18

"He who finds a wife finds a good thing, and obtains favor from the Lord."

—Proverb 18:22

"A man shouldn't tell a woman he loves her unless and until he's ready to prove it—over and over and over again."

—Marva Dew

"At the creation of man and woman, unity for them in marriage was not given as hope; it was a command! Our heavenly Father wants our hearts to be knit together. That union in love is not simply an ideal. It is a necessity."

—Henry Eyring

"Treat her like a Queen and watch those King benefits increase."

—Author Unknown

"One of my greatest days was not the day I met my wife, it was the day I FOUND her. That was the day I realized for myself that to live this life without her would be impossible."

—Dr. Gerald Dew

"Vulnerability is the unsung hero of healthy relationships."

—Author Unknown

"When a man loves a woman, can't keep his mind on nothing else. He'd trade the world for the good thing he's found."

—Percy Sledge

"The purpose of relationship is not to have another to complete you, but to have another with whom you might share completeness."

—Neale Walsch

RULE #85

When the Queen is Happy, There is Peace in the Kingdom

"It is better to live in a corner of the roof than in a house shared with a contentious woman."

—Proverb 25:24

"How do I maintain a happy, healthy, whole marriage? (1) We both work hard at it (a good marriage takes work—it

doesn't happen by happenstance; (2) I constantly ask myself, 'Marva how would you like to be married to you?' The sheer horror of the answer to that question draws me nearer to my beloved husband."

—Marva Dew

RULE #86

The Queen is Respectful of Marital Roles and Responsibilities

"Nevertheless let every one of you in particular so love his wife even as himself; and the wife see that she reverence her husband."

—Ephesians 5:33

"Success in marriage depends on being able, when you get over being in love, to really love."

—Eleanor Roosevelt

"Many marriages would be better if the husband and wife clearly understood that they are on the same side."

—Zig Ziglar

"In marriage the husband is called to love, lead, provide, and protect. The wife is called to help, manage, and love. Mutual respect is mandatory."

—Marva Dew

RULE #87

The Queen Holds Fast to the Heart and Hand of the King

"When you have a Queen [King] in your hand, don't reshuffle the deck and end up with a Joker."

—Author Unknown

"Recipe for a happy marriage: My wife and I hold hands. If I let go, she shops."

—Red Skelton

"Marriage is a thousand little things... It's giving up your right to be right in the heat of an argument. It's forgiving another when they let you down. It's loving someone enough to step down so they can shine. It's friendship. It's being a cheerleader and trusted confidant. It's a place of forgiveness that welcomes one home, and arms they can run to in the midst of a storm. It's holding on and never letting go. It's grace."

—Darlene Schacht

"At the end of my life, with just one breath left, if you come, I'll sit up and sing."

—Maulana Rumi

"An unsatisfied woman requires luxury, but a woman who is in love with a man will lie on a board."

—André Maurois

"Love at first sight is easy to understand; it's when two people have been looking at each other for a lifetime that it becomes a miracle."

—Sam Levenson

"Queen, learn to hold fast to the heart and hand of your king—lean into him. Learn to love him; believe in him; and respect him afresh every day. Learn to pray for him on a daily basis. And never lose sight of what made you fall in love in the first place. Hold his heart and his hand will follow."

—Marva Dew

RULE #88

The Queen and King Must Always Present a United Front

"If a house is divided against itself, that house cannot stand."

—Mark 3:25

"We are only as strong as we are united, as weak as we are divided."

—Author Unknown

"My husband and I are a team- two players, one team. The Bible is our playbook. When we enter the playing field of life, we do so with one voice, one mission, and one goal. We are united and as a result, we always have the strength and tenacity to win.

—Marva Dew

"There is no challenge strong enough to destroy your marriage as long as you are both willing to stop fighting against each other and start fighting for each other."

—Dave Willis

RULE #89

The Queen Has the King's Ear

"The Queen understands when she speaks the King listens. Therefore, she must protect the ear of the King even from her own voice. Pillow talk is powerful, personal, and intimate. It has the ability to build or break. The King must be able to speak privately with his Queen knowing all he has said will remain private and confidential. She, in turn, must use wisdom in responding because the King will hear her voice like none other— that can be both beautiful and dangerous. Queen, set a constant watch over your mouth. Master the art of listening. When you speak, let it be with love, understanding, and wisdom. The king will, in time, yearn for the very sound of your voice."

—Marva Dew

RULE #90

The Queen's Bed is Undefiled
Happy is the King Who Gains Satisfaction from the Queen

"Marriage should be honored by all, and the marriage bed kept pure, for God will judge the adulterer and all the sexually immoral."

—Hebrews 13:4

"Sexual intimacy is important in a marriage not only for the husband but for the wife as well. Intimacy is not purely physical. It is the act of connecting with someone so deeply you feel like you can see into their soul."

—Author Unknown

"Sometimes in marriage you don't need to talk, think, go out, or entertain others. Sometimes you have to close the door; turn on the music; dim the lights and have sex in no less than four rooms of your house."

—Marsha Highland

"Cards on the table, we're both showing hearts; risking it all, though it's hard. 'Cause all of me loves all of you..."

—John Legend

RULE #91

The Queen Knows How to Stand the Watch

"Watch and pray so that you will not fall into temptation. The spirit is willing, but the flesh is weak."

—Matthew 26:41

"I am there—waiting, watching, keeping to the shadows, but when you need me I'll step out of the shadows and protect what's mine."

—Author Unknown

RULE #92

The Queen Finds Joy in Replenishing Her Queendom

True Queens Raise New Kings & Queens

"And God blessed them, and God said unto them, 'Be fruitful and multiply, and replenish the earth, and subdue it...'"

—Genesis 1:28

"Behold, children are a heritage from the Lord, the fruit of the womb a reward."

—Psalm 127:3

"*Labor is the only blind date where you know you will meet the love of your life.*"

—Author Unknown

"*Motherhood is not a hobby, it is a calling. It is not something to do if you can squeeze the time in. It is what God gave you time for.*"

—Neila Anderson

"*Motherhood is a choice you make every day to put someone else's happiness and well-being ahead of your own; to teach the hard lessons; to do the right thing even when you're not sure what the right thing is; and to forgive yourself over and over again for doing everything wrong.*"

—Dora Bell

"*A mother's love begins before the child is born and lasts through time and difficulties, and differences, and many wounds, and days of joy, and days of sorrow—winding, wearing, weeping, sharing, changing until, at the end what remains is that solid core that began as love before the child was born.*"

— Author Unknown

"*The most precious jewels you'll ever have around your neck are the arms of your children.*"

—Author Unknown

RULE #93

The Queen Understands Family Order: God – Husband – Wife – Children

"God has an order for the family. This is about structure and responsibility, not about value."

—Kevin Smith

"Your spouse should not be second to your parents, friends, coworkers, or even your children."

—Doug Weiss

"The wife is called to submit to her husband. Submission means understanding your power and using it in a way that builds your husband's leadership."

—Juli Slattery

"She is strong and she can fight the world on her own. But that doesn't mean that she's not dreaming of resting her head on someone's shoulder. Someone, who can love a strong woman, but allow her to feel fragile and protected by his side."

—Veronika Jensen

"Don't be fooled, a submissive wife is a powerful wife—it's strength wrapped in a velvet glove."

—Marva Dew

The Queen's Rules & Royal Proclamations

The Queen Will Protect 3 Things: Her King, Her Throne, and Her Children

"Every wife and mother has a mission—to love, guide, and protect her family. Don't mess with her while she's on it."

—Vicki Reece

"She is kind but strong, and that is where so many mistake her. They interpret her kindness for weakness and force her to show her strength."

—J. M. Storm

"Because when it comes to my family I will fight with the fangs of a wolf and the claws of a dragon. And no one or nothing will stop me from protecting them."

—Jordan Weatherhead

"As women we must learn to fight on our knees for our families."

—Author Unknown

"I choose to be kind because it makes me happy. But I will defend my boundaries and my loved ones without hesitation. Make no mistake: I Am Fierce!"

—Nanea Hoffman

RULE #95

The Queen Stands Tallest When She's Standing on the Word of God

"On Christ the solid Rock I stand. All other ground is sinking sand."

—"My Hope is Built on Nothing Less"
song by Edward Mote

"I will speak of Thy testimonies also before kings, and will not be ashamed."

—Psalm 119:46

"Behold I am coming quickly. Hold fast to what you have that no one may take your crown."

—Revelation 3:11

"We must make a great difference between God's Word and the word of man. A man's word is a little sound, that flies into the air, and soon vanishes; but the Word of God is greater than heaven and earth, yea, greater than death and hell, for it forms part of the power of God, and endures everlastingly."

—Martin Luther

"There are four principles we need to maintain: first, read the Word of God. Second, consume the Word of God until it

consumes you. Third, believe the Word of God. Fourth, act on the Word of God."

—Smith Wigglesworth

"The Word of God well understood and religiously obeyed is the shortest route to spiritual perfection. And we must not select a few favorite passages to the exclusion of others. Nothing less than a whole Bible can make a whole Christian."

—Aiden Wilson Tozer

"No matter what happens in life, the Word of God will uphold you; it will sustain you; it will direct you."

—Marva Dew

RULE #96

The Queen Remains Faithful

"...Be thou faithful unto death, and I will give thee a crown of life."

—Revelation 2:10b

"Faith is an irrational leap over the need for evidence."

—John Loftus

"Surrender to what is. Let go of what was. Have faith in what will be."

—Sonia Ricotti

"Faith in God includes faith in His timing."

—Author Unknown

"Faith consists of believing when it is beyond the power of reason to believe."

—Francois Arouet

"Faith is believing BEFORE what will only make sense AFTER."

—Steven Furtick

"Have faith in God and never stop growing in faith. In order to do so one must recognize and believe in God Himself—the one true and living God. We must then (1) become serious students of the Word of God; (2) apply the Word of God to our daily lives; (3) trust God (in good or challenging times) to do what only God can do knowing that He will always do what's good, right, and best for us… that's Faith!"

—Marva Dew

A Queen has Magnetic Power— The Ability to Draw People to Her and the Courage and Wisdom to Then Drive Them to the Cross.

— Marva Dew

RULE #97

The Queen Has No Fear of the Future — God is with Her

"God is our refuge and strength, an ever-present help in trouble. Therefore we will not fear, though the earth give way and the mountains fall into the heart of the sea, though its waters roar and foam and the mountains quake with their surging."

—Psalm 46:1-3

"There is surely a future hope for you, and your hope will not be cut off."

—Proverb 23:18

"You're safe not because of the absence of danger, but because of the presence of God."

—Author Unknown

"We count on God's mercy for our past mistakes, on God's love for our present needs, and on God's sovereignty for our future."

—Saint Augustine

"God's plans for my future are far greater than my fears."

—Helen Fagan

"Your past has a way of slipping into your thoughts and inviting you to go back... back to your old ways, your old opinions, and your old habits. Your future is ahead... bright, unchallenged, and uncompromised. Keep moving forward; keep progressing; keeping growing. Use your past as a reminder of what was and an encourager of what is possible. When thinking about the future, make this your mantra—Lord I Trust You!"

—Marva Dew

"Just because the past taps you on the shoulder doesn't mean you have to look back."

—Author Unknown

RULE #98

The Queen Knows God Will Protect Her

"When you pass through the waters, I will be with you; and when you pass through the rivers, they will not sweep over you. When you walk through the fire, you will not be burned; the flames will not set you ablaze."

—Isaiah 43:2

"Whoever dwells in the shelter of the Most High will rest in the shadow of the Almighty. I will say of the LORD, He is my refuge and my fortress, my God in whom I trust."

—Psalm 91:1,2

"*The will of God will never take you where the grace of God will not protect you.*"

—Author Unknown

"*God is always doing 10,000 things in your life, and you may be aware of three of them.*"

—John Piper

RULE #99

The Queen Awaits God's
TRUE CROWNING

"*Now there is in store for me the crown of righteousness, which the Lord, the righteous Judge, will award to me on that day--and not only to me, but also to all who have longed for His appearing.*"

—2nd Timothy 4:8

"*And when the Chief Shepherd appears, you will receive the crown of glory that will never fade away.*"

—1st Peter 5:4

"*Blessed is the one who perseveres under trial because, having stood the test, that person will receive the crown of life that the Lord has promised to those who love Him.*"

—James 1:12

RULE #100

The Queen Honors Her Royal Decree & Proclamation

I DECREE and PROCLAIM...

"I am a child of the one true and living God who is King of kings and Lord of lords. I was created in the image of God. I am fearfully and wonderfully made. I believe and live according to His holy Word. I am a praying woman. I am a lead worshipper. I praise God at all times. I am loved, called, and chosen for such a time as this. I am a woman of resilience and hope. I will live a victorious life. The fruit of my womb is and will be blessed. I am blessed when I come in and blessed when I go out. I am positioned to lend to many but borrow from none. I am the head and never the tail, above and never beneath. I will live with power, purpose, passion, and praise knowing I am destined to live in victory. No weapon formed against me shall ever prosper. I am anointed and appointed. I am saved and sanctified. I wear a crown of favor. Royal blood flows through my veins. I represent God and I will faithfully serve Him all the days of my life."

— The Queen

"*Though the crown weighs heavy, wear it as if it were made of rose petals. When you sit upon the throne, sit upright in the wisdom of God. When you stand, stand weighted by the Word of God. When you reign, reign with love, peace, and compassion. When you walk, walk purposefully in strength, honor, and integrity. And when you bow, bow only to God Himself.*

You are Chosen! You are Royalty!
YOU ARE THE QUEEN!"

—Marva Dew

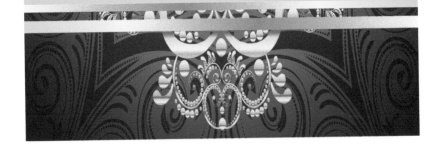

The Queen's Prayer

Heavenly Father, I bow before You in the humblest way I know how. I acknowledge Father that You are King of kings, Lord of lords, Ruler, and Master. You are Alpha and Omega, the beginning and the end. Before You there was none and after You there will be none. Father I thank You for allowing me to see a brand new day. Thank you for standing watch over me all night long. I bow in holy anticipation of what You have in store for me today. I set my heart and mind on You and You alone. Remove any wandering thoughts I might have so that I might focus solely on You. Father, forgive me of my sins—those I have committed by omission and commission. Forgive me of anything I have done that brings shame to Your name. Create in me a clean heart and renew a right spirit within me.

Father, I trust You and I trust Your timing. Thank You for opening windows and closing doors. Thank you for withholding what I'm not yet ready to receive and releasing what You see I stand in need of. Father You knew from the beginning of time where I would be at this very moment, therefore, I remove my will and ask that You do what works best for me.

Father, I thank You for Your amazing grace and undeserved favor. Thank you for choosing me as Your daughter and the apple of Your eye. Lord I believe what You, through your Word, say about me: I am fearfully and wonderfully made, I am the head and not the tail, a lender and not a borrower, blessed and highly favored. Lord I ask that you continue to transform me so that I might properly represent You. Allow me to serve You through my service to others. Your Word reminds me that You will give me the desires of my heart if I delight myself in You, therefore Lord, my heart's desire is to become a woman of prayer and a woman of Your Word. I desire to please you God and bring a smile to Your face. I desire to look like You; walk like You; talk like You; and most of all love like You. I desire to become a mirror image of You. Use me, Lord, to get for Yourself glory.

Father, help me to diligently monitor my emotions— to be quick to forgive those who offend me as You are always quick to forgive me. Whenever I become confused or lose sight of the way, help me to hasten to Your throne to find the insight, mercy, and grace I will need to do Your good work and walk victoriously in all things.

Father I thank you for a place of authority in this world. Help me Lord to use that authority for the good of others, the growth of the church, and Your glory. Keep me humble Lord, lest I get beside myself. As I fulfill my purpose in life may I do so in love at all times. May the words I speak echo your written Word. Help me to use Your gift of wisdom in all matters. And may the meditations of my heart be acceptable in Your sight at all times.

Father, I walk in the authority and power You have given me. I ask that You continue to order my steps. Speak to me and then speak through me. I love you Lord and I will bless Your holy and righteous name forever. My soul will make her boast in You alone. I seal this prayer with the hope that my humble life will somehow draw others to You and to Your blessed promise of salvation.

And now Father, in the quietness of this moment I ask that You speak to my heart Lord, your servant is listening.

In Jesus' Name I Pray This Prayer.
Amen!

My Queen Rules

_____

_____

_____

_____

_____

_____

_____

_____

_____

_____

_____